T0086246

Maa Beti

A Collection of Poems by a
Mother and a Daughter

Written and Compiled By

Gita Baksi
Mallika Sothinathan

BALBOA.PRESS
A DIVISION OF HAY HOUSE

Balboa Press books may be ordered through
booksellers or by contacting:

Balboa Press
A Division of Hay House
1663 Liberty Drive
Bloomington, IN 47403
www.balboapress.com
844-682-1282

Because of the dynamic nature of the Internet, any web
addresses or links contained in this book may have changed
since publication and may no longer be valid. The views
expressed in this work are solely those of the author and do
not necessarily reflect the views of the publisher, and the
publisher hereby disclaims any responsibility for them.

The author of this book does not dispense medical advice
or prescribe the use of any technique as a form of treatment
for physical, emotional, or medical problems without the
advice of a physician, either directly or indirectly. The intent
of the author is only to offer information of a general nature
to help you in your quest for emotional and spiritual well-
being. In the event you use any of the information in this book
for yourself, which is your constitutional right, the author and
the publisher assume no responsibility for your actions.

Print information available on the last page.

ISBN: 978-1-9822-7930-1 (sc)
ISBN: 978-1-9822-7931-8 (e)

Balboa Press rev. date: 01/29/2022

CONTENTS

DEDICATION

This book is dedicated to my Father, Sri Nisith Kumar Baksi, who departed on Jan 19th, 2021, and left a permanent void for our family. The Baksi family, The Roy family and the Sothinathans, the Soni family, and the Ralli family miss Baba dearly. You are our inspiration, Baba!

FOREWORD

From working for her to knowing her as a person, my relationship with the author of this book is respect and admiration I have for her as a person.

This book is about a relationship not discussed most often—a relationship between a daughter and her best friend for life; her mother. From knowing Mallika for almost 2-3 years, once I got the opportunity to witness the bond Mallika shares with her mother; and that made me sure that she is the one who can describe this beautiful relationship.

Writing this foreword gave me immense pleasure as I got the opportunity to read this book before it reached readers worldwide, and it made me happy to share this beautiful piece of writing with you all.

PRELUDE

This book is very special as it has precious gems. These gems are our moments together. Mom and I spent very special moments together after everyone left us after Dad passed away. Just the two of us were in the apartment, and we were discovering our lives together. My visits to India are short; by March, I return to Canada. I am not able to take the dry heat.

Interestingly this year, many people from India and Delhi in special felt a different heat. The wrath of Corona. Many families were affected, and we soon became headlines with the Delta variant. I lost 8 family and friends. We were already grieving Dad's loss, and now we had these sudden demises. Maa became clingy to her phone and kept a tab of who was with us and who wasn't. She looked lost. My brother called us and motivated us so, did all the grandsons; Mom enjoys talking to her grandson. I persuaded Mom that we needed to go to Canada as my son was waiting. Mom loves India, her plants, her friends and then she showed me her diary where she wrote her poetry. Mom loves to write Bengali poems, and she loves to recite them. The book's title is Maa beti because people in the Orchid petal colony, Gurgaon, call us by that name. This was first coined when we took our first Covid jab. Incidentally,

90 percent of the people residing here have taken the stab.

Mom has joined Toastmaster and is currently the star speaker. She has written in English too. In this book, we will share those poems. Hope you like it and enjoy!

Mallika Sothinathan

MAA
ALIAS
GITA BAKSI

I AM ALWAYS FINE

I am always fine!
Always I say I am fine
As it keeps me fine
Even when my mood is low
And I yearn for a hearty laugh
It drives away all my blues
I am fit with my happy
mood you know
One should know how
to keep oneself happy
For Happiness is only
"A State of mind"
And Happiness makes you look
Forward for brighter days.
Ahead! So be fine always

DO YOU FLY? PART 1

Do you fly?
Butterfly butterfly!
Do you fly?
High up in the sky
I see you fly near bye
In the garden in morn
When flowers bloom at dawn.
Cluttering your colorful wings.
Do you really sing?
You sit on a flower
And sip nectar with all your power.
You fly away when I run after you
And drift from flower to flower
To sip honey every hour.

DO YOU FLY? PART 2

Butterfly Butterfly!
Can you fly in the sky?
I love your colorful wings
Bright and spotted
Do you sing
To the flowers as they bloom
Early morning to drive away their glooms
Or you sip their honey
As you sit on flowers in early hours
And the flowers sway
As you say hello
All the way

TREES

Trees make the earth green
They give our life a sheen
They give us air to breath
Without trees
We would seethe
They grow flowers fruits, and food
To make our life only good
They shelter birds that sing
To make lovelier spring
Still, we cut them for our needs
And don't pay any heed
To create an imbalance in nature
With time that spoils our future
We should plant more trees
So that we don't freeze
Let us love and grow trees today
For the generations to live and stay

IN THE SCHOOL

Early morning comes Bus
To take me to school, I rush
I get ready in my uniform
For I know all the school norms
I say good morning to all I meet
For this is the way in the day we greet
We study and play with friends
All-day along we have fun
We say bye to all
As we return
To be in school
Is real fun

ON VALENTINE DAY

You stood by me
Through thick and thin
I am happy that your heart I win
You are my first and last romance
You are my hubby by chance
I admire you for your care
I love life as with you, I share
The light and darkness of life
Which has made me your wife
Fifty-four years that we share
Make us close for all the years

MY WISH

Like a squirrel, if I could jump
And take out of a cake a plum
In a hush, if I could rush
Catch a train or a bus
If I could fly
In the sky
Though I know to fly
Is to be high
I would reach you my grandson
To be with you, I know
Is real fun
On your Happy Birthday
To share the moments
I pray
I live long
To see you grow
God blesses you

BETI
ALIAS
MALLIKA
SOTHINATHAN

A POEM FOR U

Do I owe you
If I leave you
Do I owe you
If I love you
Do I owe you
If I don't feel you
Do I owe you
If I can't stand you
Do I owe you
If I hate you
Do I owe you
If I forget you
Do I owe you
If I hurt, you
Do I owe you
If I feel your pain
Do I owe you
For today tomorrow or yesterday
Do I owe you
For my life or death
Do I owe you
Or do you owe me
Forever and years to come
Do I owe you
Tell me once forever and all

JUST ME IN THE MOMENT

I will laugh I will cry
I will walk
And look up at the sky
It hurts today
But tomorrow
Will be another day
I will live
I will not die
I will survive
And smile again
I will let u go
May be u will be happy
Without me
Because it is not about me
It is about you
Your life your wish
I was just a moment
That just passed bye
Today is just the beginning
Tomorrow is the mourning
Don't shed tears for me
As it just not worth it
I was Just me in the moment
Only to be passed bye

I AM INSANE

Your smile lit my entire room
And Vanquished all my
eternal gloom
My eyes closed and the eye
lids quivered
Under the powerful gaze
As your gazed dipped in to
my face
I heard myself say stop
It hurts and tried to push away
Through the imaginary line
While you kept pushing with
all might
My tears rolled ….
And your phone was wet
True it was a call
And we were miles apart
But it was too intense
Too hard to sort
Easy to reminisce
And hard to resist
This is true love ❤
I muttered in vain
I realized I am insane

DISTANCE

Distance has brought us
Closer than ever
Yet forever fear
Engulfs us forever
Will we meet forever
Or will we part and depart
And be separate forever
Send me you picture
So that I can just see u
Send me your passion
So that I can feel u
Send me your love
So that I can be inside u
Send me your warmth
So that I can embrace u

THE FIREFLY

If I am Fire 🔥
What are you?
Who are you?
The Fire fly?
That flies innumerous
heights
Or the angel
That sways it wings
Blesses everyone
Embraces all along
Who are you?
Who am I
I feel like Fire
And you are my Firefly

EVERLASTING LOVE

Even if you stop loving me
I will continue loving you
You may ask why so?
I will say I don't know
But loving 🫠 you is a journey
Thanks for coming
And joining me in this journey
I don't expect anything
I am happy and content
And the love ♥ in my heart
Will last me a lifetime
Momentary heartache is nothing
As I am experiencing
everlasting love

TEARS IN MY EYES

I walk for miles
My child is wrapped
In my cozy arms
Her mouth is dry due to thirst
She gasps for breath
Her eyes are moist
Her head hurts in pain
Hunger has made the weak
And she clutches my chest
Tears in my eyes
I walk for miles.

My old mother walks with her stick
Her pace is not fast, nor her
walk is brisk
She looks at me
And she looks up at the skies
Hoping it rains
And drenches her pain in her veins
Tears in my eyes
I walk for miles
My heart skips

My pregnant wife weeps
Can we not go back?
To our little shack
In search of our homes
We are caught in this mess
We are the labor of a country
in stress
We are migrant labor in
distress
Tears in my eyes
I walk for miles.

IF I GO DON'T CRY

For soul stays alive
Life is just a journey
Every second we live
Just like the breeze
It passes by....
If I go don't cry.
We were friends
In a common space
Time brought us close in
the past
Time took us apart
Time may bring us
Back again
If I go don't cry

A TRIBUTE TO ALL THOSE WHO ARE GRIEVING

You tell me to be positive
That this shall pass too.
Yet every time I think
Only dark painful negative
Thoughts emerge and make me
blink
The flames of the last journey
Of many dear ones
Pain our hearts and hurt our minds
Countless tears emerge
And crumble our confidence
Be positive you say
Yet my body shivers
As we wait endlessly for negative
Covid 19 results
The vaccines are not perfect
The doctors are unsure
Medical supplies are not available
And there are many multiple
mutants
They attack us and suck out our life
My heart races in high speed
Eyes close but sleep eludes

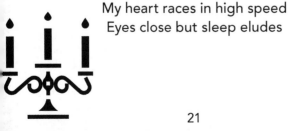

WHERE IS PEACE?

I want to seek it
While mind makes it a distant dream
Love Relationship bonding
Seem to evaporate in black smoke
And turn in mixed ashes
As I don't recognize my kin
In the last day of her life
She shared the hospital bed
She shared her pain

She finally breathed last in the shared bed
So, her ashes mingled with many
As she was tired lying for hours
Lifeless waiting for someone to pick her

Basic needs of sick are not met
Beds nor oxygen are there
The people are left to die instead
Fend for yourself!
The powerhouses say!
Bring your own oxygen bring your bed
Bring your own supplies
And your coffin or wood just in case.
As chaos emerges everywhere

You say to me Be positive
I just get bogged down with fear
I try to practice ...
But how can live without breathing!
A polluted atmosphere
A congested lung
I practice to breath
And look for fresh air...

Eat healthy, exercise, self-care
Is preached every where
But we know inside our hearts
We want to be negative and Covid free
And build a Safe distance save lives world
And Be Covid Free

THE PAIN

It hurts
Yet I see no cut
It hurts
Yet I see no blood
It hurts
Tears roll through
My closed eyes
They don't stop
Keep rolling on cheeks
I miss the beautiful voice
That called me day n night
Mithu Mithu come here
I listened sometimes
But most often was late
I sat near him
He loved clasping my hand
I held him tight
Yet he slipped away.
It hurts today.
It will hurt tomorrow.

JUST ME

Let it Be
When I lost my first love
I said to myself let it be
Let's move on
And life will move too
As years passed I failed
In school
My Juniors told me let it be
You are just older by a year
We like older women
Some brats winked and smiled in vain
A few years passed again I failed
I was not fair n lovely they said
My aunt said let it be
She will find her destiny
And fate will show her
The right way
So after just 2 decades
I said let it be
Understand the real issue
It is me
I expect too much
From me
I don't love myself
No longer can I
Let it be
It needs to be me
Just me

DEDICATED TO SENIORS
WHO LOST THEIR PARTNERS

She stood silently,
And watched him patiently.
The old eyebrows tweaked,
His eyes searched only for her
Yet his vision had a blur.

His limbs did not move
Nor did his hands,
His breath would often get caught
In a rough lengthy deep cough.

She thought she heard him,
With tear filled eyes.
She knelt towards him
Weary and tired he pushed his unsteady hands,
He clasped her safe hands
As he closed his eyes.
Only to say dear! I am right here.

Only it was just his eye movements
As no words were heard!
For an outsider
He was at hospital. On a ventilator
He had limited time,
And could meet none.

Days passed but he stayed still
His eyes did not move
Nor did he breathe
He lay lifeless
He was at peace
A lonely corpse
He is no more they said
You need to let him go

She broke down and shuddered
She said he did not go alone
He took her with her
For she was his soul

27

INSPIRED BY REJECTION

Rejections are not meant for me ...
Many a times I was told
I can't take them well
And I feel totally sold

You are not selected
You did not pass
Sorry try next time till you pass.
Some were just polite
Oh, it will happen soon don't fight!!!

Negativity and Nepotism
Are there and here to stay
Rejection letters are just
Ignition fuels for your next step.

You can do it
Just say it to yourself
And don't reject yourself
Be kind and love yourself
Opportunities will come
Positive thoughts will show you.
The right way!
Follow your heart ♥
For your passion will show you the
way.

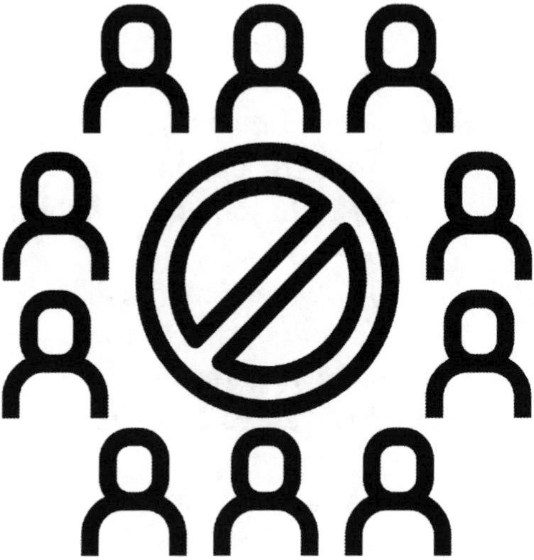

ISOLATION

I am grateful I am healthy!
I am grateful I have lots of love!
I am grateful for this life,
I am thankful to each of you,
Let's make that difference!
In some one's life.
In this confinement I have learned,
To appreciate what we have.
Let's be there for each other!
With lots of virtual hugs.
In this busy world lacking space
We often asked for space and time
Today we have it
In our locked down homes
The very space we yearned for
Self-reflection is the task here
Have we done that enough or at all?
The nature through its way showed us
Time and again we are perishable
So, hoarding wealth isn't going to take us far.
If we need to hoard, we need to hoard good deeds
Make a difference help some one
Make a smile spread happiness
Through social distancing and virtual hugs.
Saving lives is in our hands
SOOO wash Ur hands wash Ur hands
And stay in your space
And self-reflect and serve people in need.

I AM BIRD

Who likes to fly?
In the free skies
Chains and cages
Will never hold me
Your tears and love
Will move my heart
Handcuffed.

Face Down.
Knee on his neck.
They did nothing.

He called the officer "Sir."
They did nothing.

He begged for his life.
He begged for water.
He begged for mercy.
They did nothing.

His nose bled.
His body trembled.
He lost control of his bladder.
They did nothing.

He cried out, "I can't breathe."
They did nothing.

Twelve more times.

"I can't breathe."
"I can't breathe."
"I can't breathe."
"I can't breathe."
"I can't breathe."
"I can't breathe."
"I can't breathe."
"I can't breathe."
"I can't breathe."
"I can't breathe."
"I can't breathe."

They did nothing.

One last time, he gasped, "I can't breathe."
They did nothing.

He lost consciousness.
They did nothing.

A firefighter demanded they check his pulse.
They did nothing.

Off duty medical personnel begged them to stop.
They did nothing.

Deprived of oxygen.
His organs screaming.
His brain frantic.
They did nothing.
They watched George Floyd die.

His life fading.
A slow death.
They did nothing.

A lynching on the ground.
They did nothing.

For eight agonizing minutes.
Four officers watched.

He cried out for his Mom...
A grown man...
Crying out for the woman who gave him
life....
As he feared joining her in death.
And still they did nothing.
A black man.
A gentle giant.
Murdered because he was black.
And still, they've done nothing...

The officers should be arrested.
And still they've done nothing.

Rest In Peace. May justice be served.

BLACK IS HUMAN TOO, NO HUMAN
BEING IS MORE HUMAN THAN ANOTHER
HUMAN

HAPPY MOTHER'S DAY!

Unconditional love!

You brought me to this world.
And wiped my first tear.
I uttered your name, Maa...
My first word in this world.

You carried me,
Loved me spoiled me,
You laughed at me,
Cried with me.

Hid me in your safe arms
When my heart broke.
You guarded me through the night
Through the brutal fever and the cold.

You stood with pride.
Whenever you heard my name.
The laurels were mine so was my fame.
The failures were yours and you took the blame.
Yet You are on my side always.
Loving me was unconditional
Today as a mom I understand true love,
I repeat what I learned,
And try to give it all!
Thank you Maa!
For loving me 👪❤️👪
Teaching me to love and give
Thank you for being there for me
And holding my hand still.

A LETTER FROM 2005, OCTOBER

Dear Baba and Maa
I had the best time of my life this time, I came after
many years and was wondering how I will feel at
home? I truly enjoyed every moment of it

This is a little ode to you both
I may still be the impatient child
You once knew
I am still the cute chubby child
You once knew
I still the loudmouth
You once knew
I AM STILL THE CRY BABY
You once knew
I am still the emotional bundle
You once knew
A gadget destroyer
You once knew
Yes, I am your little girl
You once knew
I may not be the richest daughter
Who could send lots of cash and wine?
It is all about love and care
And I have the most
And can share
We may live in different corners of the world
But we have endless strings of love
Which never let us part
And for those who love money
Remember Money cannot buy
True love

ABOUT THE AUTHOR

MALLIKA SOTHINATHAN

is currently the Director of New Horizon Media Arts and has been associated with several TV channels in India like Zee and ETV when she was an Indian citizen. She migrated to Canada in 1999 and is a Canadian citizen. She has a Master's in Mass Communication from Mass Communication Research Centre Delhi.

She has 19 years' experience in retail, 7 years operation management and 12 years in planogram and data design and analytics. Prior to retail, she worked in the TV industry in India. She loves to write, travel and has a passion for public speaking. She has a 17-year-old son, who loves technology.

GITA BAKSI

Gita Baksi is a poet, writer a mathematician an avid read. She is post graduate in psychology from Indraprastha College, Delhi University. She is multilingual and loves to teach. She is great in IT too. She is currently pursuing Toastmasters.

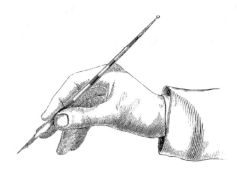

ABOUT THE EDITOR

AAKASH BHATIA

Aakash being a Content Writer, loves to write and read. From writing content for different websites to magazines; he has done a lot of work in the corporate sector. Graduated from Journalism and Mass Communication gave him the edge of knowledge with the experience of writing for different sectors of the corporate world. Other than writing, Aakash loves to travel and is exploring different Indian cities, helping him create a better and clearer perception of things.

ABOUT ILLUSTRATOR

PANKHURI PURWAR

I am Pankhuri Purwar, a student pursuing a BFA in applied arts from the College of Art, Delhi. Art has always been an important aspect of my life and often a medium of recognition and identity amongst my peers and mentors. I am a designer, and try to find a creative approach in all the work that I do while focusing on the overall aesthetics and color scheme. Balance, simplicity, and clarity are the key aspects to which I pay attention to while working on a project. Working on the book **Maa Beti** has been fun as the relationship between mother and child is very powerful and known to all.

ABOUT COVER DESIGN & GRAPHICS

MALLIKA JAIN

Postproduction Director, NHHF, India. From
Jodhpur Rajasthan (India) Completed my Bachelors
of Journalism and Mass Communications from
Noida. Since 2020 I am working in this foundation
as graphic designer and project coordinator.
I fantasy the world evolving around creativity
and to be art in the world of technology.
In this book I have tried to give my best in
graphics and designs. The idea for designing
the cover was very realistic and the digital art
was made out of real picture. I hope everyone
connect with the poems written in this book.
Cheers!!

ABOUT NEW HORIZON HOPE FOUNDATION

Founded in Mississauga, New Horizon Hope Foundation started with a handful of creative people who came together to create a feature length documentary about domestic workers in India. Over time, we realized that many social issues and stories needed to be researched, explored, and showcased to the world through the camera's eyes. With a background in journalism and media and an eye for heart-felt storytelling, we capture and make unique content on film in the form of documentaries, web series, and even corporate films. Our in-depth research, stunning cinematography, and detailed editing ensure that we create an incredible video every time.

More than anything, we are driven to creating solid content that leaves a lasting impact on viewers and has the potential to improve lives.

WWW.NEWHORIZONHOPEFOUNDATION.CA

Printed in the United States
by Baker & Taylor Publisher Services